Wild ROCK

Climbing and Mountaineering

NEIL CHAMPION

A⁺
Smart Apple Media

Published by Smart Apple Media, an imprint of Black Rabbit Books
P.O. Box 3263, Mankato, Minnesota 56002
www.blackrabbitbooks.com

Printed in the United States of America at Corporate Graphics, North Mankato, Minnesota

Library of Congress Cataloging-in-Publication Data
Champion, Neil.
 Wild rock : climbing and mountaineering / Neil Champion.
    p. cm. -- (Adventure outdoors)
 Includes index.
 Summary: "Describes the sports of rock climbing and mountaineering, along with the history of these sports. Explains the equipment needed, climbing and training techniques, and how to tie knots. Belaying, rappelling, and orienteering are also covered. Includes labels, diagrams, and reading quiz"--Provided by publisher.
 ISBN 978-1-59920-807-7 (library binding)
 1. Rock climbing--Juvenile literature. 2. Mountaineering--Juvenile literature. I. Title.
 GV200.2.C544 2013
 796.522'3--dc23
                          2011047432

Created by Appleseed Editions, Ltd.
Designed and illustrated by Guy Callaby
Edited by Mary-Jane Wilkins
Picture research by Su Alexander

Picture credits
l = left, r = right, c = center, t = top, b = bottom
Page 1 Andrey Bandurenko/Shutterstock; 2 Thinkstock; 4l Michael G Smith/ Shutterstock, r Swinner/Shutterstock; 5l Greg Epperson/Shutterstock, r Stefan Petrovski/Shutterstock; 6tl Shcherbakov Ilya/Shutterstock, tr Alysta/ Shutterstock, b Marek Cech/Shutterstock; 7t Swinner/Shutterstock, b Daniel Prudek/Shutterstock; 8l Forbis/Shutterstock, r Praseodimio/ Shutterstock; 9 & 10 Thinkstock; 11t Eric Bajart, bl Thinkstock, br Goodshot/Thinkstock;12t Michael Blann/Thinkstock, c Thinkstock, b Jupiterimages/Thinkstock; 14 Main image Shutterstock, tl Thinkstock, tr Greenland/Shutterstock, b Jan Kranendonk/Shutterstock.com; 15t & bl Grafvision/Shutterstock, br Michael Siegmund/Shutterstock; 16, 17 & 18 Thinkstock; 19 tl Jupiterimages/Thinkstock, cl Pierpaoloct, bl Hemera Technologies/ Thinkstock, r Thinkstock; 20l Scottandwendi at en.Wikipedia, r Thinkstock; 21l Stefa/Shutterstock, r Robnroll/ Shutterstock; 22 Thinkstock; 23t Trekandshoot/Shutterstock, b Iain Lees; 24t Thinkstock, b Dim Dimich/Shutterstock; 25 Thinkstock; 26 Getty Images; 27 Thinkstock; 28 Aaron Twa/Shutterstock; 29t Thinkstock; 29l Robert Ranson/Shutterstock, cl Thinkstock, cr Joe Gough/Shutterstock, r Thinkstock; 32t Worldinmyeyes.PL/ Shutterstock, b Roca/Shutterstock; Cover: Tyler Olson/Shutterstock

PO1443
2-2012

9 8 7 6 5 4 3 2 1

Contents

Let's Go Climbing!

Our planet is a very rocky place. If you put all the mountains on earth on top of each other, they'd reach beyond the moon. Why not explore them in one of the most exciting sports you can imagine—climbing.

People have been climbing for thousands of years, but only in the last 150 years have they been climbing just for the challenge and adventure. Why do they do it?

Rising to a Challenge

At first glance, climbing seems dangerous. Imagine being hundreds of feet up a sheer wall of rock a long way from safety. Your arms are aching and your legs are beginning to shake. How will you make it to the top?

This is where climbers rely on their training and skills, as well as team work. Most climbers

Two climbers tackle a sheer mountain face. The lower climber is anchored to the rock and is belaying the lead climber.

have a partner at the other end of the rope, and their limbs automatically remember how to find the next foothold. They need to keep calm and remember all the practice they've put in. That way, they'll safely reach the point on the rock face they're aiming for.

Overcoming Danger

Climbing and mountaineering appeal to our love of adventure and freedom, physical exercise, and the triumph of overcoming danger by training to deal with risk. This is what climbing is about.

Left *A partner and a thin rope stop this climber from falling.*

Amazing FACTS

Most people climb in pairs, with each person tied to one end of the rope. One climber leads, while the other lets out rope. If the leader falls, the partner holding the other end of the rope (called the belayer) holds the rope firm to catch the leader. Only when the leader has reached a safe place does the belayer start to follow.

Getting Started

You need skill to climb a rock face or scale a mountain. You can't just start climbing. New climbers need advice and training from people with years of experience.

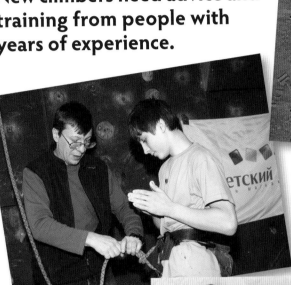

Above *A young climber takes her first steps on a climbing wall.*

Left *Learning to tie on*

You can join an outdoor club or join an organization such as the scouts or guides. Your local indoor climbing wall may have a club for young people.

TRUE Survivors

In January 2011, Adam Potter, a climber from Glasgow, survived an amazing 985 ft. (300 m) fall down a near vertical slope in Scotland almost unscathed. When mountain rescuers were sent to look for him, they feared the worst. But when they found Adam, they were astonished to discover him standing up and looking at a map. This was despite the fact that he had slipped when trying to put on **crampons** and tumbled down three rocky crags to the valley floor. Experts say he was extremely lucky to survive and even luckier to suffer only minor injuries.

Learning the Ropes

All climbers start somewhere. Clubs can lend you equipment and teach you how to use it. Here are some of the knowledge and skills climbers need.

You need to know:

- How to use a map and a compass so you can **navigate**.

- How to use equipment, such as a harness, helmet, ropes, **belay devices**, protection, and even an axe; You'll also need to use crampons for icy conditions.

- How to tie knots, including the figure eight, the clove hitch, the Italian hitch, and the overhand knot.

- About climbing and mountaineering **grades**—these tell you how hard the climb will be.

- Climbing calls, such as "Climb when ready", "Climbing", and "OK."

Amazing FACTS

Mount Everest is the highest mountain in the world at 29,029 ft. (8,848 m). The mountain is part of the Himalayas, the highest mountain chain in the world. Everest is still being pushed up a little bit every year, but it is not getting any higher. The top is being eroded (worn away) at about the same rate each year, so it stays more or less the same height.

What Type of Gear?

Climbers need to learn to use climbing equipment—from special clothing and footwear to ropes, harnesses, and helmets.

The Right Choice

All climbers need the right gear for the type of climbing they are doing. Rock boots and a chalk bag are all you need to climb indoors. Outside, you need a harness, rope, protection, **slings**, and **carabiners**, as well as a partner. Mountaineers need boots, warm waterproof clothing, a hat and gloves, a map, compass, and backpack.

Essential gear: hat and gloves, warm fleece, and sunglasses to protect eyes from the sun's glare

Modern climbers use rock boots, ropes, and metal wedges called nuts.

Amazing FACTS

A hundred years ago, climbers tied a rope around their waists in case they fell. This kind of waist loop ends up around the climber's chest and could stop them from breathing. Climbers today use a **sit harness**, which allows a climber who has fallen to sit in space and prevents the waist belt from riding up around the chest.

How Modern Ropes Work

A modern climbing rope is strong enough to hold a truck. The rope absorbs the energy of a fall by stretching, so it prevents injuries. Imagine if a **bungee jumper** jumped off a bridge attached to a metal cable. The cable would hold, but not stretch. The jumper would be injured or even killed. Jumpers use bungee cord because it works like an elastic band. It holds the climber and stretches to absorb the energy of the fall. This is what modern climbing ropes do.

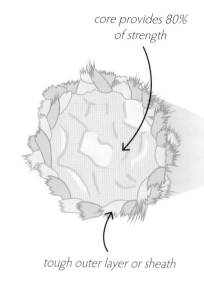

core provides 80% of strength

tough outer layer or sheath

A bungee jumper flies through the air, protected by a strong elastic cord tied to his legs.

USEFUL KNOTS

Bowline
Makes a loop at the end of a rope. Easy to untie.

Clove hitch
Attaches a rope to rock anchors or trees. Easy to untie.

Figure eight
Attaches a climbing rope to a harness. Easy to untie.

Overhand
Stops the end of a rope from unraveling. Hard to untie.

Choosing Gear

Here are some top tips to help you get started. Take advice from experienced climbers before buying or renting equipment.

Mountain Boots

🔵 **Must be comfortable and support the ankles**

When buying boots, wear climbing socks. Walk up and down a slope in the shop. Badly fitting boots lift at the heel (causing blisters) and squish your toes when going downhill.

Harness

🔵 **Should be padded and comfortable**

Some harnesses have adjustable leg loops and waist belt as well as self-locking safety buckles. They are designed to support you if you are hanging on a rope. It's important to know what sort of harness you have.

Ropes

Should be suited to specific use. If in doubt, ask an expert.

Rock Shoes

⦿ **Should fit tightly, but not squish the toes**

Rock climbing shoes have thin soles so you can feel the footholds. The sticky soles provide grip and support on the smaller footholds. Be sure that your toes lie flat and touch the inside of the shoe, but they should not be so tight that they are uncomfortable.

TRUE Survivors

Edward Whymper was desperate to be the first to reach the summit of the Matterhorn, one of the highest peaks in the Alps. He had tried and failed eight times by 1865! Whymper started his ninth attempt in July 1865 with a team of seven, including an English lord and a vicar, as well as some Swiss climbing guides. This time they reached the top. On the way down, four climbers slipped and fell to their deaths. Whymper and two guides were saved because the rope connecting them to the four who fell snapped.

Climbing Skills

Learn good techniques from the beginning. Climbers need to get up steep rock in a way that saves as much energy as possible. Fingers and arms tire first, so use your stronger feet and legs more. Good footwork, balance, and efficient movement are more important than big muscles.

A young climber uses good footwork and balance on easy angled rock.

This climber has both hands on one long, thin hold. Climbers need strong fingers!

Belaying

Belaying is a way of making sure that a climber who falls does not hit the ground. One end of a rope is fixed to a climber's harness. The rope then passes through fixed bolts or temporary fixings in the rock down to a person below, called the belayer. The belayer wears a harness with a belay device. The rope runs through the belay device and is controlled by the belayer so that the climber above cannot fall and hit the ground.

Center of Gravity

The **center of gravity** for most people is around the belly button. When we climb, we shift our center of gravity. This means we have to place one foot carefully on a hold and then put our weight over it so we can move the second foot. We can usually see holds for hands, so sometimes we put more weight on our arms than we need to.

Learning to Belay

An expert or instructor can teach you how to belay. The pictures below show you how a belay device works for a right-handed climber.

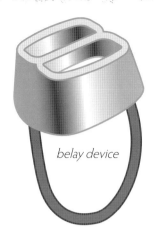

belay device

carabiner

A Thread the rope through a belay device and attach a carabiner to your harness.

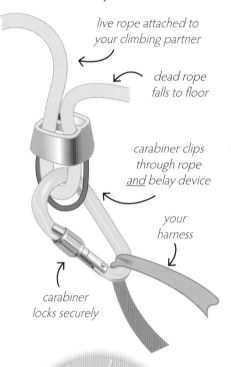

live rope attached to your climbing partner

dead rope falls to floor

carabiner clips through rope <u>and</u> belay device

your harness

carabiner locks securely

B Pull the rope, following these five steps as your climbing partner goes up.

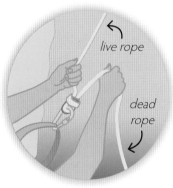

live rope

dead rope

1 With your left hand on the **live rope** and the right on the dead rope, keep the ropes parallel and pull the **dead rope**.

2 Bring the dead rope down toward your hip.

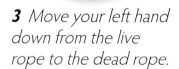

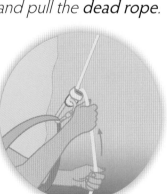

3 Move your left hand down from the live rope to the dead rope.

4 Move your right hand closer to the belay device.

5 Move your left hand back to the live rope and repeat the steps as the climber goes up.

Training Drills

Footwork and balance, rather than strong muscles, are the keys to good climbing

When you are learning to climb, concentrate on where you place your feet to take the pressure off your arms and fingers. Small moves are better than high steps or strenuous pulls. Learn to be neat with your movement and climb like a cat. Try the games on the next page at your local climbing wall to develop your technique.

Look at the body shapes of these climbers. Which look comfortable and balanced and which look as if they might be struggling?

Feet or Hands?

Once you're on the climbing wall, move in any direction—hands first, then feet. Now start again, but this time lead with your feet and then move your hands. What do you notice? Most people feel less tired when they move feet first. This is because they push up off their feet rather than pull up with their arms.

Body Shapes

Climb onto the wall and find comfortable hand and foot holds. Keep your feet where they are and move your hands to any holds you can reach—high up, to the side, or low down. What do you notice? Some of the body shapes you make will be very tiring. Now try moving just your

feet to as many different holds as you can. Body positions in which your center of gravity is farthest from your feet are more difficult.

Turn into the Wall

Climb to a vertical part of the climbing wall. Hang out from the wall with your arms straight, your feet on holds, and your body in space. After a while, your arms will tire. Pull yourself in, turning one hip to touch the wall. You should be able to stay in this position for longer because your weight is over your feet.

Amazing FACTS

The sport of slacklining started in Yosemite Valley in California in the 1970s. People walk along a climbing rope tied between two trees. The sport requires excellent balancing skills and strong muscles. Amazing feats of daring have since taken place in which a slackliner balances on a rope across a chasm hundreds of feet deep. One slip and you're gone!

Top Tips for Training

Whether you are planning to climb a high mountain or a challenging area of overhanging indoor wall, you will need to do some training. This not only helps you climb harder and longer, but it will also help you avoid injury.

Train for Success

Plan your training around the goals you want to achieve. If you want to rock climb, train at your local climbing wall. If your goal is to conquer mountains, you need to train on long walks with a heavy backpack on your back.

Strength vs. Stamina

You can build up your strength by going **bouldering**. This involves short climbs without ropes over large boulders.

Above Carrying a large backpack builds up leg muscles and stamina.

Below Short boulder climbs increase your strength and power.

16

If you practice short hard moves at the climbing wall as hard as you can, this will strengthen your short twitch muscle fibers. **Endurance** exercises build up slow twitch muscle fibers. Make up some circuits at the climbing gym, choosing easy or moderately hard moves, but keep climbing for about 10–15 minutes.

Open and Closed Skills

To play any sport well, you need to practice some of the same movements over and over again—these are called closed skills. For example, serving in tennis requires closed skills. To climb well you also need open skills. These vary depending on where you are and what is happening around you. There are many ways to climb a particular route. Climbers need to train their muscles to find the best and most efficient way to approach any climb with open and closed skills.

Amazing FACTS

Experiments have shown just how powerful our minds are when we exercise. Even thinking about physical training starts preparing your body for it. It does this by pumping chemicals into the bloodstream (for example, **adrenaline**) which help the muscles work extra hard. So you can prepare yourself for climbing by thinking about it beforehand.

Staying Safe

There can be a fine line between having an adventure in the mountains and taking dangerous risks.

Good planning, the right equipment and companions, as well as choosing a sensible route all help to make sure you have fun and stay safe. But things can still go wrong even on a well planned trip, so it's good to know what to do in an emergency.

Climbers head into the mountains to tackle a more challenging—but achievable—route they have chosen.

TRUE Survivors

In July 1977, British climbers Doug Scott and Chris Bonington stood triumphantly on top of the Ogre in Pakistan. This mountain, standing 23,900 ft. (7,285 m) is one of the hardest mountains in the world to climb. It is extremely steep and rocky, with no easy way to reach the summit.

As the climbers **rappelled** back down in the dark, Scott slipped on ice, smashed into some rocks, and broke both ankles. Then a storm blew in and the climbers were trapped high on the mountain for 24 hours. With the help of two other climbers, Scott eventually slid and crawled down to base camp.

To make matters worse, Bonington smashed two ribs and became ill with **pneumonia** during the descent. It took them eight days in all, but the climbers survived, thanks to the toughness and skills they had learned during their years of mountaineering.

Top Ten Survival Tips

1 Learn to navigate in all conditions.

2 Learn to rappel (slide down a rope).

3 Learn to read the weather.

4 Know how skilled and fit you are. Climb within your limits.

5 Learn emergency calls. The distress signal in the mountains is 6 whistle blasts or 6 light flashes in the dark. Wait one minute and start again. Rescuers give 3 blasts or flashes.

6 Learn first aid skills—they can save a life.

9 Take the right equipment and emergency food, but don't carry more than you need.

7 Learn how to make a shelter for the night anywhere.

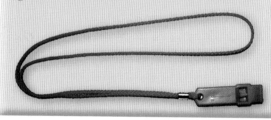

8 Learn how to find and **purify** water.

10 NEVER PANIC. In an emergency, keep calm so you can decide what to do to get to safety.

Getting Out of Trouble

Climbing and mountaineering involve risk. You need to match your experience and fitness to the climb so you can handle any dangers you meet. Then, even if something goes wrong, you can get yourself out of trouble.

Vertical caves, like the one above, and steep snow slopes are common hazards faced by mountain climbers.

TRUE Survivors

In 1992, mountaineer Colby Coombs was climbing Mount Foraker in Alaska with two friends. When a storm struck, they decided to head back down. Suddenly they were swept away by an **avalanche**. Coombs woke up dangling from his rope without his pack or mittens. He had broken his shoulder, ankle, and bones in his neck. Both his friends were dead. He spent six days scrambling painfully down to safety. Today he teaches survival skills and says, "...if you get in trouble, anything that gets in the way of success has to be eliminated—emotion, fear, pain. It's the mental things that impede survival."

Keep Cool!

A cool head is essential when you're in trouble. If you become lost on a mountain, stay calm and try to figure out where you are. Look at your map and find the last place you remember. What have you seen since leaving there? Piece together your route like a detective, then try to find the path you need on the map.

If you have to spend an unplanned night in the open, think of the important things you need to do

DID YOU KNOW?

Experiments show that if you have a positive attitude when you're in danger, it can make the difference between life and death. If you keep thinking that you'll escape eventually and reach safety or be rescued, it's more likely to happen.

to survive. Can you make a temporary home out of things around you—rock, wood, branches, or snow? Do you have anything useful in your backpack, such as a large plastic bag or sheet?

Anything that will keep out the cold night air is good. You can survive many days without food, but water is essential. Can you find any nearby? Can you purify it?

Winter Mountaineering

When snow and ice cover the mountains, you need to be able to use crampons and an ice axe. These help climbers grip the treacherous surface when even standing up can be difficult. Navigation can be difficult in the snow, where everything can look the same and there's no **horizon** to focus on.

The Right Equipment

In strong wind and freezing temperatures, the human body loses heat quickly without the right clothing. Apart from a windproof and waterproof **shell** (jacket and pants), you need two fleece or wool layers, a thermal vest and **long johns**, warm pants, and wool socks. Several pairs of gloves, a hat, and a scarf are also essential. For firm footing, you need crampons that fit on your mountain boots as well as an axe.

Steep snow and ice demand special skills, clothing, and equipment. This climber uses an ice axe and crampons to make progress.

TRUE Survivors

At around sunset on September 24, 1975, two men stood on the summit of Everest, the highest point on earth. Doug Scott and Dougal Haston had just become the first British men to scale the southwest face of the mountain. The temperature was about to drop to −40°F (−40°C), but they did not have time to reach their tent below them before dark.

They had to survive the night at over 27,890 ft. (8,500 m) up the mountain. They had no shelter, sleeping bags, or stove. They did survive, but only because they knew how to dig a makeshift **snow hole**, which gave them some protection from the harsh wind and freezing night air. Without it, they might have died or lost toes and fingers to **frostbite**.

Digging for Survival

You need to be able to dig a snow hole in an emergency to get out of the wind if you are to survive a night in a freezing landscape. Find a place where the snow is deep and has drifted, such as a hollow or the bank of a frozen stream. Use your ice axe to dig horizontally into the snow. Your hole should be big enough for you

Two mountaineers have fun digging a snow hole with two entrances.

and your backpack in a sitting position. Cut bricks of snow to block the entrance once you're inside, but make sure you leave a gap for air. Sit on your backpack or climbing rope so you're not on the frozen ground.

Finding the Way

Finding your way is a key skill. Guidebooks explain a route, but you also need to figure things out along the way.

Make sure you take all the safety gear you might need—map and compass, water and food, spare clothes, and a flashlight.

Staying Safe

Follow these rules when in the mountains:

ALWAYS LET PEOPLE KNOW WHERE YOU ARE GOING. MAKE A ROUTE CARD OR MAP.

DON'T TRAVEL ALONE.

KNOW THE ESCAPE ROUTES IF WEATHER TURNS BAD OR SOMEONE GETS SICK.

DON'T BE AFRAID TO TURN BACK.

ALWAYS TAKE A MAP, A COMPASS, AND SPARE FOOD.

LEARN TO USE GPS, BUT REMEMBER, BATTERIES RUN OUT.

Maps and Compass

A map and compass are powerful tools. Learn how to use them. The top of a map always points north and the **grid lines** go north-south and east-west. The moving arrow on a compass spins around to point to **magnetic north**. **Contour** lines show a difference in height of the land. Blue indicates water—a river, lake, or marsh. You can measure distances on your map using the ruler on the side, but you need to know the **scale** of the map.

Finding a Route

A climbing guidebook will tell you how to find the start of a route, what grade it is, and how high the climb goes. It will also tell you how to get back down. But once you start climbing, you may not remember the details. Experience helps you spot where the route goes.

Check your map regularly when you are high in the mountains so you always know where you are.

TRUE Survivors

In 2009, teenager Scott Mason was out for a day hike in the White Mountains in New Hampshire. He wanted to climb Mount Washington. However, he got lost and spent three nights out in the open. He survived to tell his tale because he was an Eagle Scout who knew how to make an emergency shelter and handle the hostile conditions. He was well equipped with warm clothing and an ice axe and crampons to deal with the snow.

Scrambling

Scrambling is a popular sport that mixes the adrenaline-rush of rock climbing with the satisfaction of getting to the top of a mountain.

As well as an easy hiking path, many rock hills and mountains have more difficult routes to the top. They may not be as hard as a true rock climb, but they still require you to use your hands as well as your feet to stay safe. Some of the hard scrambles need a rope for safety on particularly tricky and exposed parts.

A Head for Heights

Scrambling can be dangerous because many scrambles take place on easy paths but have steep drop-offs. You need a cool head. Make sure you learn to scramble with experienced people.

TRUE Survivors

In 2003, Aron Ralston was scrambling alone in Bluejohn Canyon in Utah's Canyonland National Park. A large boulder fell on his arm and trapped him. For nearly four days he tried to move it without success. When he ran out of water, he knew he would die unless he did something drastic. He cut off the trapped part of his arm with a penknife and eventually got to a place where he was spotted and rescued. Aron wrote a book about his experience, and the movie *127 Hours* is based on that book.

Three Points of Contact

Always try to keep both hands and one foot, or both feet and one hand on any rock you are scrambling up, especially if the rock is wet or slippery. Then if a hand or foot slips off, you have two other points of contact to help you regain your balance and avoid falling. Remember to keep your weight over your feet and use your legs as much as possible to push up rather than pull too heavily with your hands.

What do you know about climbing?

Are you ready to go climbing? Do you know what equipment you need, what to do if you get lost, or how to tie a clove hitch? Try this quiz and find out what you know about climbing and mountaineering. Answers are on page 31.

▼ **1** Can you match knots with their names?
a Figure eight
b Clove hitch
c Overhand knot
d Bowline

2 Which of these is a great place to learn how to climb?
a A forest
b A high mountain
c An indoor climbing wall
d A sports gym

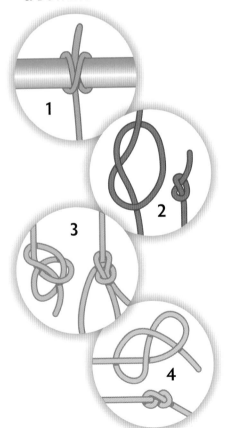

3 Which of these is true?
a Ropes stretch to absorb the energy of a falling climber.
b The belayer always climbs first.
c A sit harness means you should not stand up wearing it.
d A map is the most important navigation tool you can buy.

4 What does bouldering mean?
a Helping your climbing partner by holding the rope
b Climbing at a low level indoors or outside without a rope or special gear and using a crash mat to fall
c Running down a hillside, leaping from rock to rock
d Making piles of rock on a mountain trail to help find your way back

7 You should take crampons when you might come across:
a Wild animals
b Other mountaineers
c Thick mist and fog
d Snow and ice

5 Shell clothing is called this because:
a It is made from the shells of small sea creatures.
b It is the outer clothing a mountaineer uses to keep wind and rain out.
c It is sponsored by a well-known oil company.
d It is used only by the inhabitants of the Shell Islands.

8 Are these statements true or false?
a Dead rope means that the rope is old and you should throw it away.
b A snow hole is an emergency shelter that can be dug quickly to get out of icy conditions in the winter mountains.
c It doesn't really matter if you can navigate in the mountains, as it is not very important.
d Balance and good footwork are key to good climbing technique.

▼ **6** Match the climbing equipment to the names.
a backpack   b harness
c sling   d carabiner

1

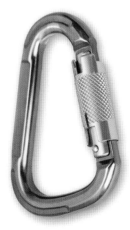

2

3

4

29

Glossary

adrenaline A chemical our bodies make to help us run from danger or fight it.

avalanche Snow that breaks away from a slope and moves fast downhill.

belay device A piece of climbing equipment that attaches to a rope and helps catch a falling climber.

bouldering Climbing at a low level without ropes, a harness, or a belay device.

bungee jump A jump off a high place attached to a bungee cord.

carabiner A metal ring used to join two things together, such as a rope and a harness.

center of gravity A point by the belly button that marks where the part of the body above weighs about the same as the part below.

contour A line on a map that shows height above sea level.

crampons Metal spikes that attach to mountain boots. They dig into snow and ice to stop climbers from slipping.

dead rope The part of a rope that comes from the belay device that is used as a brake when locked off to catch a falling climber.

endurance The aspect of fitness that allows people to continue working hard for a long time. In running, a marathon is an ultimate endurance test.

frostbite Damage done by extreme cold, usually to fingers and toes.

grade The level of difficulty of a specific climb.

grid lines Straight lines on a map that run north-south and east-west.

horizon The point where the sky meets the ground.

live rope The part of the rope that comes from the belay device and goes to the climber.

long johns A warm inner layer worn under pants.

magnetic north A place near the North Pole where compasses point to.

navigate Using a map, a compass, and natural signs to find the way around an area.

pneumonia A serious infection of the lungs.

purify To remove chemicals or bacteria from water so it is safe to drink.

rappel To slide down a rope in a controlled way.

route card A map climbers make, along with directions and notes, showing their route in case they get lost.

scale The scale of something is the relationship between its size on a map and its real size.

shell Waterproof and windproof outer clothing that protects against bad weather.

sit harness A harness with leg loops attached to a belt that keeps a falling climber in a sitting position in mid-air.

sling Strong, light supporting climbing equipment.

snow hole A shelter dug into a deep bank of snow. It can be small enough for one person or big enough to sleep ten!

Websites

American Alpine Club www.americanalpineclub.org
Mountaineers – Explore, Learn, Conserve www.mountaineers.org
USA Climbing http://usaclimbing.net

Books

Rock Climbing (Action Sports) Tom Greve, Rourke Publishing, 2009
Rock Climbing (Extreme Sports) John E Schindler, Gareth Stevens Publishing, 2005
Rock Climbing (Get Outdoors) Neil Champion, Powerkids Press, 2010
Rock Climbing: The World's Hottest Climbing Locations and Techniques (Passport to World Sports) Paul Mason, Capstone Press, 2010

Quiz answers

1

***b.** clove hitch*

***c.** overhand*

***d.** bowline*

***a.** figure eight*

2 *c*

3 *a and d are true*

4 *b*

5 *b*

6

***b.** harness*

***d.** carabiner*

***c.** sling*

***a.** backpack*

7 *d*

8 *a false   b true   c false   d true*

Index